HAIKUS OF ALL SEASONS IV

FLORA

MAYUMI ITOH

For the souls of flowers

and

Eliza Ruhamah Scidmore (1856–1928)

the initial proponent for transplanting

Japanese flowering cherry trees to

Washington, D.C., which was realized in 1912

Contents

Note for paperback edition: This book is for on-demand printing. The actual page numbers (and page breaks and other formatting matters) may differ from the page numbers shown in the Table of Contents above, due to the formatting by Amazon that is used on the day of the book order.

List of photographs

All photographs were taken by the author except for those whose sources are credited below.

Photograph 1. Pink ornamental kale (*ha botan, lit.,* "leaf peony")

Photograph 2. Purple crocuses with snow

Photograph 3. Tsubaki (camellia), "Camellia japonica 'Fukutsuzumi,'" March 14, 2015, under Creative Commons license,

https://upload.wikimedia.org/wikipedia/commons/c/c7/Ca mellia_japonica_%27Fukutsuzumi%27_._椿_福鼓 (ふくつ づみ)_%2816626508399%29.jpg

Photograph 4. Weeping cherry blossoms

Photograph 5. American flowering dogwood blossoms

Photograph 6. Yellow irises by the lake

Photograph 7. Japanese flowering dogwood blossoms

This book presents each haiku in both Japanese and English so that non-Japanese-speaking readers can fully appreciate it. The first page for a given haiku (on the left side) shows the original haiku in Japanese, which is made up of a combination of Chinese characters (*kanji*) and Japanese phonetic characters (*hiragana* and *katakana*). In accordance with the customs for writing haiku, the old spellings of *hiragana* are used for the original haiku.

Then, in order to facilitate a better understanding, especially for those who are studying Japanese, the original haiku is shown in a modern spelling in *hiragana* and *katakana*. This allows readers to see how the haiku is exactly pronounced phonetically. There are many ways to pronounce specific *kanji* words, and the original Japanese haiku does not indicate how each *kanji* word is actually pronounced. It is sometimes difficult even for Japanese readers to know the pronunciation. Therefore, the simpler

rendition of each haiku only in modern *hiragana* and

katakana will help.

Afterward, the identification of the season word for

the haiku is given and some explanations of the cultural and

historical backgrounds are added where applicable.

On the second page for a given haiku (on the right

side), a romanization of the original Japanese haiku is

provided, first, so that English-speaking readers can

understand how the haiku is pronounced. The words in

Roman letters are divided into smaller groups of syllables,

for easier reading.

Then, an English translation of the haiku is

presented. It is a paraphrasing of the haiku, rather than a

literal translation, in order for it to make the best sense in

English. Accordingly, for many cases, the word order of

the haiku might be different from the original haiku in

Japanese. It is followed by the English translations of the season word and the explanations of the cultural and historical backgrounds. This completes the presentation of a given haiku.

All translations, including those of haikus, were made by the author. For romanizing Japanese words, the Hepburn style is primarily used, with macrons. However, macrons are not used for words known in English without macrons, as for Kyoto and Tokyo. Another exception is that "n" is not converted to "m" for words where it precedes "b, m, and p." Examples include tonbo, instead of tombo; Gunma prefecture, instead of Gumma prefecture; and tanpopo, instead of tampopo.

Names of Japanese persons are given with the surname first, except for those who use the reversed order in English. Honorific prefixes, such as doctor and mister, are not used in the text, except in direct quotations.

Acknowledgments

I would like to thank all the members of *Hoshi no shima kukai* (the Haiku Society of Star Island, a new name for the Haiku Society of New York), past and present—including but not limited to Esaka Kinuyo, Hara Yasuko, Sakuhara Aya, and Tsukino Popona—as well as Tsuneo Akaha, Kent Calder, Toshiko Calder, Steve Clemons, Akiko Collcutt, Gerald Curtis, Joshua Fogel, Ronald Hrebenar, Ken Kawata, Donald Keene, Ellis Krauss, Mike Mochizuki, T. J. Pempel, Stephen Roddy, Gilbert Rozman, Richard Samuels, Vicki Wong, Donald Zagoria, and Quansheng Zhao, for continuous encouragement and inspirations. I extend my deep appreciation to Gregory Rewoldt and Meg Itoh for generous support.

Preface

This is the fourth haiku anthology by this author and
embraces one of the seven themes of haiku: flora. As
background information, this book introduces anecdotes
about the culture and history of flowers, where applicable.
This book is dedicated to the souls of flowers in general,
and particularly to those of cherry blossoms, as the latter
represent flowers in Japan. This anthology is also a tribute
to the people who have devoted themselves to the
preservation of flora and its natural environment, including
Eliza Ruhamah Scidmore (1856–1928), the initial
proponent for transplanting Japanese flowering cherry trees
to Washington, D.C., which materialized in 1912. It is no
exaggeration to state that few people understood and
appreciated Japanese culture and nature as profoundly as
she did at that time.

For rules about haiku making, please see *Haikus of All Seasons I: The Heavens and The Earth* (2018). For details of the life and works of Eliza Ruhamah Scidmore, please read: *Eliza Ruhamah Scidmore and Japan: The Life and Journeys to the Far East of the American Woman Who Brought "Sakura" to Washington, D.C.* (2017).

162th birthday of Eliza Ruhamah Scidmore

October 14, 2018

January

Photograph 1. Purple ornamental kale (*ha botan*, "leaf peony"), taken by the author

葉牡丹の無き

　　異国の門や

　　　　ニュー・イヤー

はぼたんのなき

　　いこくのもんや

　　　　ニュー・イヤー

季語　　葉牡丹（冬）　ニュー・イヤー（新年）

厳密に言えば、季重なりとなるが、この句の場合、二つの

季語が補完し合っており、齟齬がないので許容される。門

松にも使われ、冬の風物詩である葉牡丹が、門や玄関に

飾られていない異国の正月を寂しく思う気持ち。

Ha botan no naki

    ikoku no mon ya

        Nyū iyā

New Year's Day

    without ornamental kale

        at the entrance gate in a foreign country

Season words: *ha-botan* (*lit.*, "leaf peony," ornamental

kale; signifies winter) and *Nyū iyā* (New Year's Day;

signifies the new year)

This has double season words, but, in this case the two

compliment each other without conflicting, which is acceptable.

Ornamental kale is a ubiquitous presence in Japanese gardens in

the winter when few flowers bloom. It is a must for the new

year to adorn the entrance gate of a residence and a building.

福寿草

　　赤き鼻緒の

　　　　止まりけり

ふくじゅそう

　　あかきはなおの

　　　　とまりけり

季語　福寿草(新年)

福寿草は、元日草とも言われる。

Fukujusō

   akaki hanao no

      tomari keri

The adonis

   the girl's red sandal strings

      have stopped moving

Season word: *fukujusō* (*lit.*, "fortune and longevity plant,"

adonis; new year)

Another name for *fukujusō* is *ganjitsu-sō*, which means the

new year's day plant. The red sandal strings refer to straps

for wooden clogs traditionally worn by girls.

室の梅

　　　ひっそりと

　　　　　ひっそりと待つ

むろのうめ

　　　ひっそりと

　　　　　ひっそりとまつ

季語　　室の梅（冬）

正月用などに、室で早咲きさせた梅を室咲（むろざき）の

梅と言う。

Muro no ume

> hissori to

>> hissori to matsu

The plum tree in the hot house

> is waiting

>> patiently and quietly to bloom

Season word: *muro no ume* (plum tree in a hot house; winter)

Plum trees are forced to bloom in hot houses for the new year or other occasions.

冬桜

　　雪より生まれ

　　　　雪に消ゆ

ふゆざくら

　　ゆきよりうまれ

　　　　ゆきにきゆ

季語　冬桜（冬）　雪（冬）

Fuyu zakura

    yuki yori umare

        yuki ni kiyu

The winter cherry blossom

    is born out of snow

        and disappears in snow

Season words: *fuyu zakura* (winter-blooming cherry; winter) and *yuki* (snow; winter)

The winter cherry has smaller white blossoms than those of the spring cherry.

六花

　　天の手紙を

　　　　届けたり

むつのはな

　　てんのてがみを

　　　　とどけたり

季語　六花（むつのはな、雪の結晶、冬）

六花（むつのはな）は、雪の雅語。雪の結晶が六角形であ
ることに由来する。「雪博士」として知られる北海道大学の
中谷宇吉郎（1900年−1962年）は、二つとして同じ形の
ない、変化無限の水晶細工のような雪の結晶を「天から送
られた手紙である」としてその解読・解明に勤しんだ。

Mutsu no hana

    ten no tegami o

       todoke tari

The six-petalled crystal flower

    has delivered

       the letter from Heaven

Season word: *mutsu no hana* (*lit.*, "six-petalled flower,"

refers to snowflake; winter)

Nakaya Ukichirō (1900–1962) at Hokkaiō University

pioneered the scientific classification of snow crystals and

produced the first artificial snow crystals in 1936. He

wrote that "Snow crystals are letters sent from Heaven."

天よりの

　　手紙読む

　　　六花の窓辺

てんよりの

　　てがみよむ

　　　りくかのまどべ

季語　六花（りくか、雪の結晶、冬）

六花（りくか）は六花（むつのはな）の別の呼び方。中谷宇吉郎は、大雪山系の十勝岳の山小屋「白銀荘」で雪の結晶を観測し、また、北海道大学の実験室で1936年、世界で初めて、人工の雪の結晶を作るのに成功した。

Ten yori no

tegami yomu

rikuka no madobe

At the window with six-petalled crystal flowers

one is reading

the letter from Heaven

Season word: *rikuka* (*lit.*, "six-petalled flower," refers to

snowflake; winter)

Nakaya Ukichirō observed snow crystals (snowflakes) at

Mount Tokachi of the Daisetu Mountain Volcanic Group in

Hokkaidō. He is referred to as the "Snow Doctor."

沖縄の

　　北から咲くや

　　　　寒緋桜

おきなわの

　　きたからさくや

　　　　かんひざくら

季語　　寒緋桜（冬）

寒緋桜の別名は、元日桜。沖縄で１月から咲く。沖縄の

寒緋桜は、寒くなると咲く。従って、本州では通常、北上す

る桜前線に対して、北から咲く。

Okinawa no

   kita kara saku ya

      kanhi zakura

The kanhi cherry tree

   blooms from the north

      in Okinawa

Season word: *kanhi zakura* (kanhi cherry tree; winter)

The kanhi cherry tree blooms in Okinawa in January from the north, unlike on the Japanese main island, where cherry trees bloom from the south to the north.

紅型の

　　羽織紡ぎて

　　　　緋寒桜

びんがたの

　　はおりつむぎて

　　　　ひかんざくら

季語　緋寒桜（冬）

緋寒桜は、寒緋桜の別称。紅型（びんがた）染めは、沖縄

の伝統工芸。

Bingata no

    haori tsumugi te

        hikan zakura

The hikan cherry tree

    looks as if it were weaving

        the bingata jacket

Season word: *hikan zakura* (hikan cherry tree; winter)

The hikan cherry tree is another name for the kanhi cherry

tree. The bingata is the traditional resist-dyeing method in

Okinawa characterized by bright colors and bold patterns.

白水仙

　　神の衣を

　　　　纏ひたり

しろずいせん

　　かみのころもを

　　　　まといたり

季語　白水仙（冬）

Shiro zuisen

kami no koromo o

matoi tari

The white daffodil

is wearing

the clothes of the gods

Season word: *shiro zuisen* (white daffodil; winter)

ナルキッサス

　　自己陶酔の

　　　　白き息

ナルキッサス

　　じことうすいの

　　　　しろきいき

季語　　ナルキッサス(冬)

ギリシア神話のナルキッサスの逸話。

Narukissasu

jiko tōsui no

shiroki iki

The narcissus

the white breath

of self-love

Season words: *narukissasu* (narcissus; winter)

This is based on the story of Narcissus in Greek mythology.

February

Photograph 2. Crocuses with snow, taken by the author

黄蠟梅

　　貴夫人の香の

　　　　匂ひ立つ

きろうばい

　　きふじんのかの

　　　　においたつ

季語　黄蠟梅（冬）

Ki rōbai

ki fujin no ka no

nioi tatsu

The yellow wintersweet blossoms

the scent of the noble lady

permeates the air

Season word: *ki-rōbai* (yellow wintersweet, Japanese

allspice; winter)

クロッカス

　　根雪布団の

　　　　重さかな

クロッカス

　　ねゆきぶとんの

　　　　おもさかな

季語　クロッカス(春)　根雪(冬)

この句では、クロッカスが主季語で、根雪は副次的な季語
として使われている。二つの季語が補完し合い、齟齬して
いないので、この季重なりは許容範囲と見なされる。

Kurokkasu

    neyuki buton no

        omosa kana

The crocus

    is feeling the weight

        of the pile of frozen snow

Season words: *kurokkasu* (crocus; spring) and *neyuki* (pile of frozen snow; winter)

Neyuki is used as an auxiliary season word in this haiku and does not contradict with the main season word, *kurokkasu*.

雪割草

　　　天使の羽を

　　　　　広げたり

ゆきわりそう

　　　てんしのはねを

　　　　　ひろげたり

季語　　雪割草（春）

早春に咲く、白、ピンク、紫色の可憐な雪割草は、まるで

天使のようである。

Yukiwari sō

tenshi no hane o

hiroge tari

The liverleave

is spreading

the wings of an angel

Season word: *yukiwari-sō* (*lit.*, "snow-breaking plant,"

liverleave, *hepatica nobilis*; spring)

Liverleave has dainty flowers in white, pink, and purple.

堅香子の

　　花に眠れる

　　　　雪の精

かたかごの

　　はなにねむれる

　　　　ゆきのせい

季語　堅香子（かたかご、春）

堅香子（かたかご）は、片栗の古名。薄紫色の百合のよう

な形をした清楚な小花が、下を向いて咲く。

Katakago no

hana ni nemureru

yuki no sei

In the flower of the fawnlily

sleeps

the spirit of the snow

Season word: *katakago* (*katakuri*, Asian fawnlily, dogtooth

violet; spring)

Katakago is the archaic name for *katakuri* (Asian fawnlily).

Its elegant flower looks like a small lily in pale purple.

白馬村

　　堅香子揺らす

　　　　シャッターの音

はくばむら

　　かたかごゆらす

　　　　シャッターのおと

季語　堅香子（かたかご、春）

堅香子（かたかご）は、片栗（カタクリ）の古名。カタクリは、

夏は登山、冬はスキーで知られる長野県白馬村の「村の

花」。清楚な花をカメラに収めようと観光客が早春に訪れる。

Hakuba mura

katakago yurasu

shattā no oto

In Hakuba village

the sound of the camera shutter

makes the fawnlily blink

Season word: *katakago* (*katakuri*, Asian fawnlily; spring)

Katakago is the archaic name for *katakuri* (Asian fawnlily).

It is the official flower of Hakuba village, Nagano

prefecture. Tourists visit the village in February, in order

to take pictures of this delicate flower.

東風吹かば

　　梅の匂ふや

　　　　天満宮

こちふかば

　　うめのにおうや

　　　　てんまんぐう

季語　東風（春）　梅（春）

太宰府に左遷された菅原道真（845年–903年）の短歌、
「東風吹かば　匂ひ起こせよ　梅の花　主人無しとて　春を
忘るな」へのオマージュ。

Kochi fuka ba

    ume no niou ya

        Tenman gū

When the east wind blows

    it carries the scent of plum blossoms

        to Tenman Shrine

Season words: *kochi* (east wind in the spring; spring) and

ume (plum blossoms; spring)

This is a homage to Sugawara no Michizane (845–903), who

wrote a famous poem, "On the east wind let you plum blossoms

send your scent so that you will remember the spring even

without your master." He was exiled to Dazaifu (current

Fukuoka) from Kyoto, the ancient capital of Japan. Sugawara

was posthumously deified and enshrined in Tenman Shrine.

飛梅や

　　主人偲びて

　　　　東風となり

とびうめや

　　あるじしのびて

　　　　こちとなり

季語　飛梅（春）　東風（春）

太宰府に左遷された菅原道真にまつわる太宰府天満宮
の「飛梅」伝説。

Tobi ume ya

    aruji shinobi te

        kochi to nari

The plum blossoms

    have missed their master

        and became the east wind and flew

Season words: *tobi ume* (flying plum blossoms; spring)

and *kochi* (east wind in spring; spring)

This refers to the legend of Sugawara no Michizane, in which the

white plum tree missed him so much that it flew all the way to

Dazaifu from Kyoto. There actually stands a venerable 1,000-

year old "flying plum tree" at Tenman Shrine in Dazaifu, which

blooms first in the season among the plum trees at the shrine.

白梅や

　　白寿重ねて

　　　　いと美しき

しらうめや

　　はくじゅかさねて

　　　　いとはしき

季語　白梅（春）

美し（はし）は、文語読みで、「美しい」という意味。一方、
美し（いし）と読むと、「良い、好ましい」という意味となる。

Shira ume ya

hakuju kasanete

ito hashi ki

The white plum

has grown to be several hundred years old

and is still very beautiful

Season word: *shira ume* (white plum; spring)

楊貴妃と

　　謂ふ名の梅の

　　　　謂れあり

ようきひと

　　いうなのうめの

　　　　いわれあり

季語　　梅（春）

Yō Kihi to

　　iu na no ume no

　　　　iware ari

The plum

　　called Yō Kihi

　　　　has its own story

Season word: *ume* (plum; spring)

This species of plum is named after the Chinese imperial

consort, Yang Guifei (719–756). The Japanese

pronunciation of Yang Guifei is Yō Kihi.

山茱萸や

　　いにしへの香の

　　　　綻びて

さんしゅゆや

　　いにしえのかの

　　　　ほころびて

季語　山茱萸の花(春)

山茱萸(さんしゅゆ)は、黄色の小花を咲かせ、その芳香で虫を誘き寄せる。秋には、「秋珊瑚」と言われるほど鮮やかな実をつける。

Sanshuyu ya

inishie no ka no

hokorobi te

The cornelian cherry blooms

and the scent of ancient time

emerges

Season word: *Sanshuyu* (Japanese cornelian cherry,

Japanese cornel, Asiatic dogwood; spring)

The fragrance of its dainty yellow flowers attracts insects.

March

Photograph 3. Tsubaki (camellia), "Camellia japonica 'Fukutsuzumi,'" March 14, 2015, under Creative Commons license, https://upload.wikimedia.org/wikipedia/commons/c/c7/Camellia_japonica_%27Fukutsuzumi%27_._椿_福鼓（ふくつづみ）_%2816626508399%29.jpg

白椿

　　焔となりて

　　　　燃えにけり

しろつばき

　　ほのおとなりて

　　　　もえにけり

季語　　白椿（春）

母の火葬式の様子。

Shiro tsubaki

    honō to nari te

        moe ni keri

The white camellia

    has turned into fire

        and burned away

Season word: *shiro tsubaki* (white camellia; spring)

This is an image of my mother's cremation.

三十郎

　　椿の川を

　　　　待ち佗びし

さんじゅうろう

　　つばきのかわを

　　　　まちわびし

季語　　椿（春）

黒沢明の映画「椿三十郎」（1962年）は、椿が象徴的意味合いを持ち、侍屋敷の泉水から流れる落椿が襲撃の合図として効果的に使われた。

Sanjūrō

    tsubaki no kawa o

        machi wabishi

Sanjūrō

    is patiently waiting for

        the camellias floating on the brook

Season word: *tsubaki* (camellia; spring)

Sanjūrō, the protagonist in the film "Tsubaki Sanjūrō" (1962) by Kurosawa Akira, effectively used floating camellias on a brook as the sign for the attack on the residence of a corrupt official during the Edo period.

白椿

　　デュマの亡霊

　　　現わるる

しろつばき

　　デュマのぼうれい

　　　あらわるる

季語　白椿（春）

アレクサンドル・デュマ・フィス（1824年−1895年）の長編小説、『椿姫』にちなんで。ジュゼッペ・ベルディがこの原作を元にオペラ La Traviata（椿姫）を作曲した。

Shiro tsubaki

Duma no bōrei

arawa ruru

In the white camellia

the soul of Dumas fils

appears

Season word: *shiro tsubaki* (white camellia; spring)
Dumas fils refers to Alexandre Dumas fils (1824–1895),
who wrote the semi-autobiographical novel *La Dame aux
caméllias* (The Lady of the Camellias), which was turned
into a play and then was adapted for Giuseppe Verdi's
opera, *La Traviata* (The Fallen Woman).

紅つばき

　　椿寿祝ひの

　　　　紅をさす

べにつばき

　　ちんじゅいわいの

　　　　べにをさす

季語　紅つばき(春)

椿寿(ちんじゅ)は、長寿を意味する。その由来は、『荘子
逍遥遊』中の一節、「上古に大椿なる者有り、八千歳を以
て春と為なし、八千歳を以て秋となす」。中国で紅椿という
木は、椿ではなく、異なる木。

Beni tsubaki

    chinju iwai no

        beni o sasu

The red camellia

    is celebrating her thousand-year birthday

        and puts on the gift of red lipstick

Season word: *beni tsubaki* (red camellia; spring)

The camellia is known for its longevity. The Chinese philosopher Zhuangzi (Zhuang Zhou, circa 369BC–circa 286BC) wrote that there was an 8,000-year-old camellia in ancient times.

盆石の

　　　白雲流れ

　　　　　落椿

ぼんせきの

　　　しらくもながれ

　　　　　おちつばき

季語　　落椿（春）

Bonseki no

shira kumo nagare

ochi tsubaki

The white clouds flow

on the miniature rock garden on the tray

and the camellia falls

Season word: *ochi tsubaki* (falling camellia; spring)

Bonseki (*lit.*, "tray stones") is the art of miniature landscape

making on a tray using sand and stones.

夫婦椿

　　お札連なる

　　　　八重垣神社

めおとつばき

　　おふだつらなる

　　　　やえがきじんじゃ

季語　夫婦椿（春）

島根県松江市にある八重垣神社は、素盞嗚尊と櫛名田比
売を祀り、縁結びの神社として有名。夫婦椿は、二つの根
元が繋がって一本の幹となっていることからの命名。

Meoto tsubaki

o fuda tsura naru

Yaegaki jinja

The couple camellia tree

at Yaegaki Shrine

layers of prayer tags are tied on

Season word: *meoto tsubaki* (couple camellia tree; spring)

The couple camellia tree is so called because it has two trunks at

the bottom, but they are joined together and form one tree. This

symbolizes a good marriage. Yaegaki Shrine in Matsue,

Shimane prefecture, enshrines the God Susano'o and the

Goddess Princess Kushinada, who were a married couple. Thus,

the shrine is dedicated to marriage and matchmaking.

信濃路に

　　春を告げたり

　　　　山辛夷

しなのじに

　　はるをつげたり

　　　　やまこぶし

季語　春（春）　山辛夷（春）

小説家、堀辰雄（1904年−1952年）の短編「辛夷の花」
に寄せて。随筆集、『大和路・信濃路』（1943年）の一編。

Shinano ji ni

   haru o tsuge tari

      yama kobushi

The kobushi magnolia

   is informing the Shinano Road

      of the arrival of spring

Season words: *haru* (spring; spring) and *yama kobushi*

(kobushi magnolia; spring)

The kobushi magnolia has smaller white flowers, whereas

the common magnolia has larger purple flowers. The

writer Hori Tatsuo (1904–1953) wrote essays about the

Shinano Road in Nagano prefecture, one of which was

titled, "*Kobushi no haha*" ("The kobushi magnolia," 1943).

山辛夷

　　雪の雫と

　　　　見紛へて

やまこぶし

　　ゆきのしずくと

　　　　みまがえて

季語　山辛夷（春）

堀辰雄は、短編「辛夷の花」を「そのまつしろい花からは、いましがたの雪が解けながら、その花の雫のやうにぽたぽたと落ちてゐるにちがひなかった。」と結んでいる。

Yama kobushi

yuki no shizuku to

mimagae te

The kobushi magnolia blossoms

are mistaken

for drops of melting snow

Season word: *yama kobushi* (kobushi magnolia; spring)

This is an image after the closing passage of the essay

"*Kobushi no haha*" ("The kobushi magnolia," 1943) by

Hori Tatsuo.

三椏や

　　「金の花」には

　　　　意味二つ

みつまたや

　　きんのはなには

　　　　いみふたつ

季語　三椏(春)

ミツマタは、春に芳香のある黄色い花を咲かせる。その樹皮は和紙の原料となり、紙幣にもなることから、「金の花」と呼ばれる。

Mitsumata ya

>   kin no hana niwa

>   imi futatsu

The Oriental paperbush

>   has two reasons

>   for being called "gold flower"

Season word: *mitsumata* (Oriental paperbush, mitsumata; spring)

The Oriental paperbush has fragrant, golden yellow flowers in clusters. Its bark fibres are durable and are used to make traditional Japanese paper, including banknotes. Hence it is called "gold flower."

催花雨や

　　ゆるる蕾の

　　　　嬉しかり

さいかうや

　　ゆるるつぼみの

　　　　うれししかり

季語　催花雨（春）

Saikau ya

yururu tsubomi no

ureshi kari

The early spring rain

the loosening flowering buds

must be happy

Season word: *saika-u* (*lit*., "rain that induces plants to

bloom," early spring rain; spring)

April

Photograph 4. Weeping cherry blossoms, taken by the author

薄墨桜

　　　千年寄り添ふ

　　　　　白き風

うすずみざくら

　　　せんねんよりそう

　　　　　しろきかぜ

季語　薄墨桜（春）

岐阜県本巣市の根尾谷にある有名な薄墨桜。日本三大
巨桜の一つで、国の天然記念物である。

Usuzumi zakura

    sen nen yorisou

      shiroki kaze

The Usuzumi cherry tree

    has been tended by the white wind

      for a thousand years

Season word: *Usuzumi zakura* (*lit.*, "pale sumi-ink cherry tree"; spring)

The flowers of this *Edo higan* (an early bloomer) change their color from pale pink, to white, and then to gray (*usu zumi*, pale sumi-ink); hence the name. This 1,500-year old cherry tree in Motosu, Gifu prefecture, is said to have been planted in person by Emperor Keitai (450?–531?). It was designated as a Natural Monument of Japan in 1922 and was resuscitated in 1950.

太閤の

　　枝垂れ桜や

　　　　里帰り

たいこうの

　　しだれざくらや

　　　　さとがえり

季語　枝垂れ桜（春）

2018年4月1日、豊臣秀吉（1537年−1598年）ゆかりの「太閤枝垂れ桜」のクローンの苗木の植樹式が、秀吉生誕の地、現在の名古屋市中村区中村公園で行われた。

Taikō no

    shidare zakura ya

      sato gaeri

The flowering weeping cherry

    of Taikō Hideyoshi

      has made a homecoming

Season word: *shidare zakura* (flowering weeping cherry; spring)

On April 1, 2018, a sapling cloned from the flowering weeping cherry in Daigo Temple in Kyoto that Taikō (the title for the retired Imperial Regent) Toyotomi Hideyoshi (1537–1598) had admired was transplanted to his birth house, current Nakamura Park in Nagoya, Aichi prefecture.

花冷や

　　紅き蕾の

　　　　悴みて

はなびえや

　　あかきつぼみの

　　　　かじかみて

季語　花冷(春)

Hana bie ya

akaki tsubomi no

kajikami te

On the cold spring day

the red bud of the cherry tree

has shrunk

Season word: *hana bie* (a cold day in the cherry blossom

season; spring)

シドモア桜

　　外人墓地の

　　　　守となり

シドモアざくら

　　がいじんぼちの

　　　　もりとなり

季語　シドモア桜（春）

「シドモア桜」は、イライザ・シドモア（1856年−1928年）の

発案・提唱により、1912年にワシントンに植樹された桜の

子孫のことをさす。神奈川県横浜市にある外人墓地にシド

モアの母と兄（在横浜米国総領事）の墓があり、そこに「シ

ドモア桜」が植えられている。

Shidomoa zakura

Gaijin bochi no

mori to nari

The Scidmore cherry tree

has become the caretaker of

the Foreign Cemetery

Season word: *Shidomoa zakura* (Scidmore cherry tree;

spring)

Eliza Ruhamah Scidmore (1856–1928) was the initial proponent for

transplanting Japanese flowering cherry trees to Washington, D.C.,

which materialized in 1912. The "Scidmore cherry trees" refer to

the trees that were grafted from the 1912 trees. One of them stands

at the grave of her mother and brother (the U.S. consul general) in

the Foreign Cemetery in Yokohama, Kanagawa prefecture.

荘川桜

　　湖底の民の

　　　　息遣ひ

しょうかわざくら

　　こていのたみの

　　　　いきづかい

季語　　荘川桜(春)

1952年、高碕達之助(1885年−1964年)は、電源開発初代

総裁として、岐阜県荘川の御母衣ダム建設に着手したが、住民

の猛反対に遭う。長年の説得の末、1960年に住民の同意を得

た。その際、湖底に沈む予定の集落の寺にあった桜の老木二

本を集落の「記憶」として救うことに決めた。桜の植樹は不可能

であると言われたが、奇跡的に成功し、「荘川桜」と命名された。

Shōkawa zakura

    kotei no tami no

        iki zukai

The Shōkawa cherry tree

    listens to the breaths

        of the people at the bottom of the lake

Season word: *Shōkawa zakura* (Shōkawa cherry tree, of

the *Azuma/Edo higan* species; spring)

In 1952 when the Japanese government began the project for the

Mihoro Dam in the Shō River in Gifu prefecture, the villagers

protested, as the 1,200 residents would lose their home. Takasaki

Tatsunosuke (1885–1964), president of Japan Electric Power

Development, in the end obtained their consent. He decided to save the

two 500-year-old cherry trees at the village temples as mementos of the

community that was to sink in 1960. The transplanting was considered

impossible but the trees budded the next spring and exist today.

花筏

　　　萬の願ひを

　　　　　運びたり

はないかだ

　　　まんのねがいを

　　　　　はこびたり

季語　花筏（春）

Hana ikada

    man no negai o

        hakobi tari

The cherry blossom raft

    is carrying

        ten thousands wishes

Season word: *hana ikada* (cherry blossom raft; spring)

Cherry blossom petals that fall on the river float like a raft.

周恩来の

　　詠みし「さ・く・ら」よ

　　　　嵐山

しゅうおんらいの

　　よみしさ・く・らよ

　　　　あらしやま

季語　　さくら（春）

1919年4月、日本留学を半ばで断念し、帰国した周恩来
（1898年−1976年）は、帰途、京都に立ち寄り、最後の
花見を楽しんだ。嵐山で2句、円山（まるやま）公園で2句、
それぞれ趣の深い詩を書いた。

Shū Onrai no

yomi shi "sa ku ra" yo

Arashiyama

Zhou Enlai wrote poems

about "sa ku ra"

in Arashiyama

Season word: *sakura* (cherry blossoms; spring)

The Chinese leader Zhou Enlai (1898–1976) visited

Arashiyama and Maruyama Park in Kyoto, in April 1919,

on his way home from his study years in Japan. He was

taken by the fragile beauty of the cherry blossoms and

wrote four poignant poems about them on his departure.

花吹雪

　　仁和寺の回廊

　　　夢巡る

はなふぶき

　　にんなじのかいろう

　　　ゆめめぐる

季語　　花吹雪（春）

京都の仁和寺は、かつては御室御所と称された名刹であ
る。兼好法師（吉田兼好、1283年頃−1352年頃）の『徒
然草』に登場する「仁和寺にある法師」の話は、ユーモア
に富み、教訓も含んでいて興味深い。

Hana fubuki

Nin'na ji no kairō

yume meguru

The cherry blossom shower

dreams are circling

in the corridor of Nin'na Temple

Season word: *hana fubuki* (*lit.*, "cherry blossom shower,"

falling cherry blossoms; spring)

Nin'na Temple is one of the most venerable and respected

temples in Kyoto. An interesting episode about a monk in

this temple is compiled in *Tsurezure gusa* (Idle Essays) by

Kenkō hoshi (Yoshida Kenkō, circa 1283–circa 1352).

十六日桜

　　古今の俳人

　　　鼓舞したり

じゅうろくにちざくら

　　ここんのはいじん

　　　こぶしたり

季語　十六日桜（じゅうろくにちざくら、春）

愛媛県松山市にある伝説の山桜。伊予の国の侍であった老翁が重体になり、「子供の頃から親しんできた庭の桜の花を見てから死にたい」と言うので、その息子が桜に祈ったところ、旧正月の16日（陰暦）に桜が咲いたという伝承から、「十六日桜」と呼ばれる。別名、「孝子桜」。芭蕉、一茶、子規などの俳人がこの桜を詠んだ。この古木は戦災で焼けたが、その子孫が現存する。

Jūroku nichi zakura

kokon no haijin

kobu shitari

The Sixteenth-day cherry tree

has inspired many haiku writers

past and present

Season word: *Jūroku-nichi zakura* (*lit.*, "sixteenth-day

cherry tree"; spring)

This refers to a legendary cherry tree in Matsuyama, Ehime

prefecture. A dying old samurai in Iyo province wished to see

cherry blossoms in his garden before he died. His son prayed to

the cherry tree to grant his father's wish. Then, the tree

blossomed on January 16 in the lunar calendar; hence the name.

The tree was burned during World War II, but its offspring exist.

十六桜

　　ロシアの捕虜を

　　　　慰めて

じゅうろくざくら

　　ロシアのほりょを

　　　　なぐさめて

季語　十六桜（じゅうろくざくら、十六日桜、春）

小泉八雲（ラフカディオ・ハーン）の『怪談』の中の「十六桜」の再話は、
「伊予の国の侍であった老人が庭の桜の木が枯れてしまったのを嘆き、
自分の命と引き換えに桜に命を与えるため切腹した」、とある。日露戦
争（1904年−1905年）中、松山市にはロシア人俘虜収容所があり、
地元住民が手厚く待遇した。将校は広い邸宅に住み、外出も自由で、
道後温泉や花見・観劇を楽しんだ。下級兵士は寺の宿坊に住み、海
水浴や観光旅行もした。第二次世界大戦後、日本人捕虜が極寒のシ
ベリアで強制労働に従事させられたのとは雲泥の差であった。

Jūroku zakura

Roshia no horyo o

nagusame te

The Sixteenth-day cherry tree blossoms

console

the Russian prisoners of war

Season word: Jūroku *zakura* (*lit.*, "sixteenth-day cherry tree"; spring) The story of this cherry tree as told by Lafcadio Hearn (Koizumi Yakumo, 1850–1904) in *Kwaidan: Stories and Studies of Strange Things* (1904) goes: An old samurai in Iyo committed harakiri suicide in order to resuscitate the old cherry tree by giving his own life to the tree. During the Russo-Japanese War (1904–1905), a concentration camp for Russian POWs was created in Matsuyama. Local folk treated them generously so that Russian officers lived in a large house, went out freely, and enjoyed the Dōgo Hot Springs and theaters, while lower-rank soldiers lived in temple lodgings and went to the beach and on excursion trips. This made a stark contrast to the Russian treatment of the Japanese POWs who were interned in Siberia after World War II.

May

Photograph 5. American flowering dogwood blossoms,

taken by the author

ハナミズキ

　　日米友好

　　　繋ぎたり

ハナミズキ

　　にちべいゆうこう

　　　つなぎたり

季語　ハナミズキ（春）

ハナミズキは、1912年、当時の東京市長尾崎行雄（憲政
の神様、議会政治の父、1858年−1954年）のソメイヨシノ
2,000本の寄贈の返礼に米政府が1915年に東京に贈っ
た日米関係ゆかりの木。

Hana mizuki

Nichi bei yūkō

tsunagi tari

The American flowering dogwood

has tied the knot

of friendship between Japan and the United

States

Season word: *hana mizuki* (American flowering dogwood;

spring)

The U.S. government sent the American flowering

dogwoods to Tokyo in 1915, in return for the gift of

Japanese flowering cherry trees in 1912, which resulted in

the National Cherry Blossom Festival in Washington, D.C.

花水木

　　胡蝶となりて

　　　　空と消え

はなみずき

　　こちょうとなりて

　　　　そらときえ

季語　花水木(春)

Hana mizuki

kochō to nari te

sora to kie

The American flowering dogwood

has become a butterfly

and disappeared into the air

Season word: *hana mizuki* (American flowering dogwood;

spring)

平等院

　　鳳凰の吹く

　　　　藤の風

びょうどういん

　　ほうおうのふく

　　　　ふじのかぜ

季語　藤（春）

京都府宇治市にある平等院は、鳳凰堂で有名であるが、

樹齢300年になる4株の藤がある。藤棚に1メートル余りの

長さの花房が1万8千本も垂れ下がり、芳香を放つ。

Byōdō in

    Hō ō no fuku

       fuji no kaze

Byōdō-in

    the phoenix is spreading

       the scent of the wisteria

Season word: *fuji* (wisteria; spring)

The Byōdō-in in Uji, Kyoto prefecture, is famous for its

Phoenix Hall, a National Treasure of Japan, which a pair of

golden phoenixes adorn. On the premises, four 300-years-

old wisterias bloom, with 18,000 gorgeous flower racemes

(clusters) of more than three-feet long each, hanging from

the terrace, emitting a fragrant scent.

紫木蓮

　　　恥じらひの色

　　　　　開きたり

しもくれん

　　　はじらいのいろ

　　　　　ひらきたり

季語　紫木蓮(春)

Shi mokuren

hajirai no iro

hiraki tari

The purple magnolia

opens itself up

bashfully

Season word: *shi mokuren* (purple magnolia; spring)

紫木蓮

　　　オキーフの

　　　　　化身のごとく

しもくれん

　　　オキーフの

　　　　　けしんのごとく

季語　紫木蓮（春）

画家ジョージア・オキーフ（1887年−1986年）の作品を連
想して。

Shi mokuren

   Okiifu no

      keshin no gotoku

The purple magnolia

   blooms as if it were

      an incarnation of O'keeffe

Season word: *shi mokuren* (purple magnolia; spring)

O'keeffe refers to the American artist Georgia O'keeffe
(1887–1986).

春驟雨

　　連翹の黄の

　　　　いや増して

はるしゅうう

　　れんぎょうのきの

　　　　いやまして

季語　春驟雨（春）　連翹（春）

驟雨（しゅうう）は、激しく降るにわか雨のこと。

Haru shū u

    rengyō no ki no

        iya mashi te

The spring rain shower

    makes the forsythia look

        even more yellow

Season words: *haru shū-u* (spring rain shower; spring) and

rengyō (forsythia; spring)

菜の花や

　　　静御前の

　　　　　舞ひ舞台

なのはなや

　　　しずかごぜんの

　　　　　まいぶたい

季語　菜の花(春)

静御前の霊が菜の花に乗り移ったという伝承と静御前の

霊が菜摘女に乗り移るという世阿弥作の謡曲「二人静(ふ

たりしずか)」にちなんで。

Na no haha ya

Shizuka gozen no

mai butai

The rapeseed blossoms

watch

Lady Shizuka dancing

Season word: *na no haha* (rapeseed blossoms; spring)

This is an image of Shizuka Gozen (1169?–1192?), the

famed court dancer and consort of the tragic warrior

Minamoto no Yoshitsune (1159–1189), after Zeami's Nōh

play, Futari Shizuka (two Shizukas), in which the soul of

Lady Shizuka transferred to a rapeseed blossom picker.

星粒を

　　大地に散らす

　　　　繁縷かな

ほしつぶを

　　だいちにちらす

　　　　はこべかな

季語　繁縷(ハコベ、春)

Hoshi tsubu o

daichi ni chirasu

hakobe kana

The chickweed is blooming

as if tiny stars were scattered

on the earth

Season word: *hakobe* (common chickweed; spring)

天国の

　　菫の丘に

　　　　游ぶ母

てんごくの

　　すみれのおかに

　　　　あそぶはは

季語　菫(春)

Tengoku no

    sumire no oka ni

        asobu haha

The mother

    is playing in the field of violets

        in Heaven

Season word: *sumire* (violet; spring)

アヴィニョンの

　　橋で踊るよ

　　　　花ヴィオラ

アヴィニョンの

　　はしでおどるよ

　　　　はなヴィオラ

季語　花ヴィオラ（春）

フランス童謡「アヴィニョンの橋」に寄せて。楽器のヴィオラ
と区別するため、「花ヴィオラ」とした。

Avinyon no

    hashi de odoru yo

      hana viora

On the Avignon Bridge

    the viola blossoms

      are dancing

Season word: *hana viola* (viola, miniature pansy; spring)

This is inspired by the French song, Sur le Pont d' Avignon

(On the Avignon Bridge) composed in the 15th century.

This bridge on the Rhone River still exists today.

June

Photograph 6. Yellow irises by the lake, taken by the author

杜若

　　業平卿の

　　　　霊佇みて

かきつばた

　　なりひらきょうの

　　　　れいたたずみて

季語　杜若（カキツバタ、夏）

『伊勢物語』にある在原業平（825年－880年）のカキツバ
タの短歌に寄せて。業平は、現在の愛知県知立市の八橋
で有名なカキツバタの短歌を書いたと言われる。

Kaki tsubata

Narihira kyō no

rei tatazumi te

In the field of irises

the soul of Ariwara no Narihira

stands

Season word: *kaki tsubata* (Japanese iris; summer)

The aristocrat and poet, Ariwara no Narihira (825–880),

wrote a poignant poem about the iris in Yatsuhashi (*lit.*,

"eight bridges") in current Chiryū, Aichi prefecture, which

was compiled into the *Ise monogatari* (The Tale of Ise).

花菖蒲

　　茅葺き屋根の

　　　花冠

はなしょうぶ

　　かやぶきやねの

　　　はなかむり

季語　花菖蒲（夏）

イライザ・シドモア（1856年−1928年）は、1880年代に初来日した際、農村地帯ののどかな田園風景に魅了され、とりわけ、アヤメが茅葺き屋根の上に植えられていたことに感動した。水仙や花菖蒲を茅葺き屋根に植えることは、その美しさのみならず、屋根を補強するという重要な機能を果たしていた。

Hana shōbu

   kaya buki yane no

      hana kamuri

The irises

   adorn the thatched roof

      like a tiara

Season word: *hana shōbu* (Japanese iris; summer)

In the mid-1880s, Eliza Ruhamah Scidmore (1856–1928) was taken by the beauty of the Japanese countryside in which the local folk had planted irises on a thatched roof. Planting irises and lilies actually made the foundation of the roof more durable, thus offering strength, as well as beauty to the house.

石楠花や

　　女人高野の

　　　　吐息聴く

しゃくなげや

　　にょにんこうやの

　　　　といききく

季語　石楠花（夏）

女人高野として知られた奈良県宇陀市にある室生寺は、石楠花の名所としても有名。境内には、無数の石楠花がひっそりと咲く。

Shakunage ya

    Nyonin Kōya no

        toiki kiku

The rhododendron

    is listening to the sighs

        of the Nyonin Kōya

Season word: *shakunage* (rhododendron; summer)

Murō Temple in Uda, Nara prefecture, is known for

rhododendron. This temple is referred to as the Nyonin Kōya

(Kōya for Women). The Kongōbu Temple on Mt. Kōya,

founded by Kūkai (774–835), did not allow women, as with most

temples. Murō Temple was open to women, and women who

had suffered domestic violence took refuge there.

長谷寺や

　　牡丹座りて

　　　　コンテスト

はせでらや

　　ぼたんすわりて

　　　　コンテスト

季語　　牡丹(夏)

奈良県桜井市にある長谷寺は、牡丹の名所。美人の典型
を表現した、「立てば芍薬、座れば牡丹、歩く姿は百合の
花」の言い伝えより連想。

Hase dera ya

    botan suwari te

        kontesuto

At Hase Temple

    peonies are sitting primly

        and are having a beauty contest

Season word: *botan* (tree peony, as opposed to *shakuyaku*, herbaceous peony; summer)

Hase Temple in Sakurai, Nara prefecture, is famous for gorgeous tree peonies. A Japanese saying refers to a beautiful woman as, "She looks like a herbaceous peony when she stands up, she looks like a tree peony when she sits down, and she looks like a lily when she walks."

満天星

　　大龍寺に咲く

　　　天の川

まんてんせい

　　だいりゅうじにさく

　　　あまのがわ

季語　満天星（灯台躑躅、どうだんつつじ、夏）

満天星は、灯台躑躅（どうだんつつじ）の別称。岐阜県岐阜市粟野にある大龍寺の本堂を灯台躑躅の白い花が包み込む様子は天の川に例えられている。

Manten sei

Dairyū ji ni saku

ama no gawa

The manten-sei blossoms

at Dairyū Temple

look as if the Milky Way is flowing

Season word: *manten-sei* (*lit.*, "million stars in the sky,"

refers to *dōdan tsutsuji, enkianthus perulatus*; summer)

Dairyū Temple in Gifu, Gifu prefecture, has 1,000 prized

dōdan tsutsuji bushes, with bell-shaped white flowers,

encircling its main hall. This is likened to the Milky Way.

水芭蕉

　　念仏唱へる

　　　　座禅仏

みずばしょう

　　ねんぶつとなえる

　　　　ざせんぼとけ

季語　水芭蕉（夏）

水芭蕉の黄緑色の花穂を包む純白の仏炎苞は、文字通り、

仏様が座って念仏を唱えているようである。

Mizu bashō

nenbutsu tonaeru

zazen botoke

The mizu-bashō

is the sitting Buddha

chanting the sutra in the marsh

Season word: *mizu-bashō* (*lit.*, "aquatic Japanese banana,"
Asian/white skunk cabbage; summer)
The Oze Marsh in Oze National Park, spanning Gunma and
Fukushima prefectures, is known for a colony of aquatic
mizu-bashō, with distinctive white bracts, which suggest a
miniature Pure Land of Paradise. It is a popular destination
for moderate hiking.

振り向けば

　　薔薇の囁き

　　　　森の呼ぶ

ふりむけば

　　ばらのささやき

　　　　もりのよぶ

季語　薔薇(夏)

Furimuke ba

    bara no sasayaki

        mori no yobu

Turning back

    one hears the whispers of the rose

        and the invitation of the wood

Season word: *bara* (rose; summer)

野中の薔薇

　　シューベルトの

　　　　調べ香りたり

のなかのばら

　　シューベルトの

　　　　調べ香りたり

季語　薔薇（夏）

ゲーテ（1749年―1832年）の詩にシューベルト（1797年
―1828年）が曲をつけた歌曲『野ばら』（Op. 3-3　D257）
に寄せて。

Nonaka no bara

Shūberuto no

konsāto

The rose in the field

is listening to the concert of

Schubert

Season word: *bara* (rose; summer)

This is a homage to the lied, Heidenröslein (Rose on the Heath), Op. 3-3, D. 257, by Franz Schubert (1797–1828), based on the poem by Jonathan Wolfgang von Goethe's (1749–1832).

ブルーポピー

　　ヒマラヤの

　　　幻の青ひらく

ブルーポピー

　　ヒマラヤの

　　まぼろしのあおひらく

季語　ブルーポピー（ヒマラヤ青芥子、夏）

ヒマラヤに咲くブルーポピーは、「幻の花」と言われる。

Brū popii

Himaraya no

maboroshi no ao hiraku

The blue poppy

the illusionary blue of the Himalayas

blooms

Season word: *blue poppy* (Himalayan blue poppy;

summer)

The Himalayan blue poppy is an elusive flower and is

called "an illusionary flower."

青芥子や

　　難民の越えし

　　　　山と空

あおけしや

　　なんみんのこえし

　　　　やまとそら

季語　青芥子（ヒマラヤ・ブルーポピー、夏）

1950年以来、中国政府の弾圧を受けたチベット人が難

民となり、ヒマラヤ山脈を越えてインドに逃亡した。ダライ・

ラマ14世（1935年生まれ）もしかり。そして、インド北部、

ダラムサラにチベット亡命政府を樹立した。

Ao keshi ya

    nanmin no koeshi

        yama to sora

The blue poppy

    watches the mountains and the sky

        where the Tibetan refugees crossed

Season word: *blue poppy* (Himalayan blue poppy;

summer)

Persecuted by the Chinese government since 1950, Tibetan

refugees, including the 14th Dalai Lama (b. 1935), crossed

the Himalayas to flee to India. Dharamshala, India, became

an asylum for the Tibetan refugees, and the 14th Dalai

Lama established the Government of Tibet in Exile there.

July

Photograph 7. Japanese flowering dogwood blossoms,

taken by the author

山法師

　　弁慶坊の

　　　　仁王立ち

やまぼうし

　　べんけいぼうの

　　　　におうだち

季語　　山法師（夏）

山法師の力強い枝振りと白い花が、弁慶とその白い裏頭
（かとう、弁慶頭巾）を彷彿させる。

Yama bōshi

Benkei bō no

Niō dachi

The Japanese flowering dogwood

stands as if Benkei were striking

a daunting pose of Niō

Season word: *yama bōshi* (Japanese flowering dogwood; summer)
The Japanese flowering dogwood signifies summer, whereas the
American flowering dogwood signifies spring. The Japanese
dogwood has a sturdy appearance and its white flower reminds one
of the white head cover (*katō*) of the warrior monk. The warrior
monk Benkei (?–1189?) served the tragic warrior Minamoto no
Yoshitsune. Niō refers to the pair of wrathful and muscular
guardians of Buddha placed at the entrance gate of temples.

滑莧

　　小さき命

　　　　弾けたり

すべりひゆ

　　ちいさきいのち

　　　　はじけたり

季語　　滑莧（すべりひゆ、ハナスベリヒユ、夏）

スベリヒユ（common purslane, *portulaca oleracea*）の花言

葉は「いつも元気」。よくポーチュラカ（マツバボタン、moss

rose, *portulaca grandiflora*）と混同される。前者は、多年草

で、葉は長円形の多肉質、花は一重。一方、後者は、一

年草で、針のような尖った葉をつけ、八重咲きもある。

Suberi hiyu

    chiisaki inochi

        hajike tari

The purslane

    has popped up

        its tiny lives

Season word: *suberi hiyu* (common purslane, *portulaca oleracea*; summer)

In the language of flowers, purslane means "always lively." *Suberi hiyu* (common purslane, *portulaca oleracea*) is often mistaken for portulaca (moss rose, *portulaca gladiflora*). The former is a perennial, with oval-shaped succulent leaves and single-petal flowers. The latter is an annual, with pointed leaves, and some species have double-petal flowers.

鈴蘭や

　　微かな風の

　　　　声の色

すずらんや

　　かすかなかぜの

　　　　こえのいろ

季語　鈴蘭（夏）

Suzu ran ya

    kasuka na kaze no

        koe no iro

The lily of the valley

    looks as if it were the faint color

        of the voice the gentle wind

Season word: *suzuran* (lily of the valley; summer)

夏椿

　　世の儚さを

　　　　憂ひたり

なつつばぎ

　　よのはなかさを

　　　　うれいたり

季語　夏椿（夏）

夏椿の別名は、シャラノキ（沙羅樹）。仏教の聖樹である沙羅樹（サラノキ）に擬せられてこう呼ばれる。その白椿のような美しい花は、一日で落花する「一日花」である。

Natsu tsubaki

    yo no hakanasa o

        urei tari

The summer camellia

    laments

        the ephemeral nature of the world

Season word: *natsu tsubaki* (summer camellia, Japanese
stewartia; summer)

This medium sized deciduous tree, native to Japan, grows
white flowers in summer, which resemble white camellias
and bloom only for a day.

立葵

　　独り待ちたる

　　　　無人駅

たちあおい

　　ひとりまちたる

　　　　むじんえき

季語　立葵（夏）

Tachi aoi

hitori machi taru

mujin eki

The hollyhock

waits for someone alone

at the unmanned station

Season word: *tachi aoi* (hollyhock; summer)

君子蘭

　　一葉一葉を

　　　　撫でし母

くんしらん

　　ひとはひとはを

　　　　なでしはは

季語　君子蘭（受咲き君子蘭、ウケザキクンシラン、夏）

Kunshi ran

hito ha hito ha o

nadeshi haha

The clivia

the mother used to clean its leaves gently

leaf by leaf

Season word: *kunshi ran* (*lit.*, "nobleman's orchid," *clivia miniate*, bush lily; summer)

This plant has distinctive glossy leaves and striking orange flowers.

モネ探ね

　　睡蓮橋に

　　　　足を停め

モネたずね

　　すいれんばしに

　　　　あしをとめ

季語　　睡蓮（夏）

フランス印象派の画家、クロード・モネ（1840年−1926年）

の代表作の一つ、「睡蓮の池と日本の橋」（1899年）は、

プリンストン大学の美術館に所蔵されている。同大1883

年の卒業生で、メトロポリタン美術館長であったウィリアム・

チャーチ・オズボーンが所有していたもの。

Mone tazune

    suiren bashi ni

        ashi o tome

In search of Monet

    one stops

        at the water lily bridge

Season word: *suiren* (water lily; summer)

Monet refers to the French Impressionist painter Claude Monet

(1840–1926), whose works includes "Water Lilies and the

Japanese Bridge (1899)," housed at the Princeton University Art

Museum. It is from the Collection of William Church Osborn—

Class of 1883 of Princeton University, trustee of Princeton

University (1914–1951), and president of the Metropolitan

Museum of Art (1941–1947)—and was given by his family.

「幻のモネ」

　　見つけ睡蓮の

　　　安堵せり

まぼろしのモネ

　　みつけすいれんの

　　　あんどせり

季語　睡蓮（夏）

2017年、第二次世界大戦中にフランス政府が敵対財産
として没収した「松方コレクション」に含まれていた「睡蓮
柳の反映」がパリのルーブル美術館で発見された。「松方
コレクション」は、戦後松方家に返還され、上野西洋美術
館に寄贈されたが、その一部の行方は不明であった。今
回発見された油彩画が、「睡蓮　柳の反映」であると判明。

"Maboroshi no Mone"

mitsuke suiren no

ando seri

The lost Monet

was found

and the water lily is relieved

Season word: *suiren* (water lily; summer)

In September 2016, the "Water Lilies with Reflections of a Willow

Tree" (1916) that Matsukata Kōjirō (1866–1950), prime minister/

finance minister Matsukata Masayoshi's son and president of

Kawasaki Shipbuilding, had purchased from Monet in person was

discovered in the Louvre Museum in Paris. It was part of the

Matsukata Collection that had been confiscated by the French

government during World War II and went missing afterward.

バーベナや

　　手毬の唄ふ

　　　　万華鏡

バーベナや

　　てまりのうたう

　　　　まんげきょう

季語　バーベナ(夏)

Bābena ya

    temari no utau

        mange kyō

The verbena blooms

    like a kaleidoscope

        of embroidered handballs for children

Season word: *vābena* (verbena; summer)

The *temari* is an embroidered handball made by hand-
stitching of multi-colored threads into unique abstract
patterns. Traditionally, it was used as a children's toy, but
today it is used for interior decoration, as an art craft.

カリブラコア

　　　無数の鐘を

　　　　　揺らしたり

カリブラコア

　　　むすうのかねを

　　　　　ゆらしたり

季語　　カリブラコア（夏）

赤、黄、ピンク、紫、白の愛らしい小花をつけるカリブラコ
アの別称は、ミリオン・ベル。

Kariburakoa

    musū no kane o

        yurahsi tari

The calibrachoa

    is ringing

        countless bells

Season word: *kariburakoa* (calibrachoa; summer)

The calibrachoa is also called million bells.

August

Photograph 8. Pink morning glory after the rain, taken by

the author

緋のダリア

　　世の不条理を

　　　　怒りたり

ひのダリア

　　よのふじょうりを

　　　　いかりたり

季語　ダリア（夏）

Hi no daria

   yo no fujōri o

      ikari tari

The red dahlia

   is enraged

      by the unreasonable world of people

Season word: *daria* (dahlia; summer)

蓮の露

　　御仏様を

　　　　潤して

ハスのつゆ

　　みほとけさまを

　　　　うるおして

季語　　蓮(夏)

Hasu no tsuyu

mi hotoke sama o

uruoshi te

The lotus dew

is quenching

the thirst of Buddha

Season word: *hasu* (lotus; summer)

姫早百合

　　俯向くやうに

　　　　挨拶し

ひめさゆり

　　うつむくように

　　　　あいさつし

季語　姫早百合（ヒメサユリ、オトメユリ、夏）

ヒメサユリは、薄いピンクの花をつける。横向きに咲き、甘い芳香を放つ。

Hime sayuri

    utsumuku yō ni

        aisatsu shi

The princess lily

    greets

        shyly

Season word: *hime sayuri* (*lit.*, "princess lily," *lilium rubellum*; summer)

This species of lily, native to Japan, blooms with pale pink flowers, which have a sweet fragrance.

白馬村

　　百合のパレット

　　　青き空

はくばむら

　　ゆりのパレット

　　　あおきそら

季語　百合（夏）

長野県白馬村などのスキー・リゾートでは、夏場に利用さ
れていないゲレンデを色とりどりの百合の花畑に転用して、
夏の観光地として誘致している。

Hakuba mura

yuri no paretto

aoki sora

In Hakuba village

the field of lilies spreads like a palette

under the blue sky

Season word: *yuri* (lily; summer)

Ski resorts, such as Hakuba village, Nagano prefecture,

plant lilies on ski slopes, as a summer tourist attraction.

青楓

　　　色づく時を

　　　　　　指折り数へ

あおかえで

　　　いろづくときを

　　　　　ゆびおりかぞえ

季語　青楓（夏）

Ao kaede

iro zuku toki o

yubi ori kazoe

The green maple

is counting on its fingers

the days until it turns red

Season word: *ako kaede* (green maple; summer)

夏の空

　　ポプラそびえる

　　　恵迪寮

なつのそら

　　ポプラそびえる

　　　けいてきりょう

季語　ポプラ（セイヨウハコヤナギ、夏）

ポプラの和名は、西洋箱柳（セイヨウハコヤナギ）。1903

年に日本で最初にポプラの植えられた北海道大学のポプ

ラ並木は有名。同大の学生寮の一つである恵迪寮（けい

てきりょう）は、その歴史を1876年に遡る。

Natsu no sora

    popura sobieru

        Keteki ryō

In the summer sky

    the poplar is soaring

        by the Keiteki Dormitory

Season word: *natsu no sora* (summer sky; summer)

Hokkaidō University, in Sapporo, Hokkaidō, has a famous avenue of poplars that originated in the first poplars planted in Japan in 1903. The Keiteki-ryō, a historic dormitory of the university, dates back to 1876.

月下美人

　　　薄命の

　　　　　夜想曲弾く

げっかびじん

　　　はくめいの

　　　　　やそうきょくひく

季語　月下美人(夏)

月下美人は、稀にしか咲かず、さらに、咲く時には一夜の
みしか咲かないことから、「美人薄命」の代名詞としてふさ
わしい。

Gekka bijin

hakumei no

yasōkyoku hiku

The queen of the night

is playing the nocturne

of the short life

Season word: *gekka bijin* (*lit.*, "beauty under the moon,"
queen of the night, *epiphyllum oxypetalum*; summer)

This gorgeous white flower blooms rarely, and only for one
night when it does.

向日葵七つ

　　ファン・ゴッホと

　　　　対話する

ひまわりななつ

　　ファン・ゴッホと

　　　　たいわする

季語　　向日葵（夏）

徳島県鳴門市にある大塚国際美術館は、世界の有名な

絵画や美術品の原寸大の陶板複製画を製作し、展示して

いる。その中には、システィーナ礼拝堂、「ゲルニカ」、「最

後の晩餐」の他に、フィンセント・ファン・ゴッホ（1853年−1

890年）の描いた油彩画「向日葵」の全7点がある。

Himawari nanatsu

 fan Gohho to

  taiwa suru

The seven sunflowers

 are conversing

  with van Gogh

Season word: *himawari* (sunflower; summer)

The Ōtsuka Museum of Art in Naruto, Tokushima prefecture, is

a unique art museum specializing in a collection of full-size

ceramic reproductions of major works of art in the world,

including the Sistine Chapel and Guernica, as well as the Last

Supper by Leonardo da Vinci and all of the seven paintings of

"Sunflowers" by Vincent van Gogh (1853–1890).

朝顔や

　　幼稚園児の

　　　　添ひ寝して

あさがおや

　　ようちえんじの

　　　　そいねして

季語　朝顔（秋）

Asagao ya

yōchien ji no

soine shite

The morning glory

is taking an afternoon nap

with the kindergartners

Season word: *asagao* (morning glory; autumn)

名古屋朝顔

　　袴姿の

　　　　内裏入り

なごやあさがお

　　はかますがたの

　　　　だいりいり

季語　朝顔（秋）

「名古屋朝顔」は、人の顔ほどの大輪の花、切り込み入り

の花、斑入りの葉など様々な特徴のある品種。毎年、名古

屋城公園で催される品評会に展示された見事な名古屋朝

顔は、袴を履いて御殿に参内した宮廷人が勢揃いして、

並んでいるように見える。

Nagoya asagao

    hakama sugata no

        dairi iri

The Nagoya morning glory

    is entering the palace

        wearing formal trousers

Season word: *asagao* (morning glory; autumn)

The Nagoya morning glory is known for its exceptionally

large size, colorful patterns, and variegated leaves.

Exhibition and jury contests are held annually in the

Nagoya Castle Park in Nagoya, Aichi prefecture. *Hakama*

are traditional formal trousers worn by the nobility.

September

Photograph 9. White mukuge (Korean rose, *hibiscus syriacus*), taken by the author

無窮花や

　　利休の懐ふ

　　　　高麗の女

むきゅうかや

　　りきゅうのおもう

　　　　こうらいのひと

季語　　無窮花（木槿、秋）

無窮花は、木槿の韓国名。木槿は、韓国の国花である。

山本兼一（1956年–2014年）原作の千利休（1522年–1

591年）の伝記小説、『利休にたずねよ』（2008年）より。

Mukyūka ya

Rikyū no omou

Kōrai no hito

The *mukyūka* remembers

the Korean woman

that Rikyū loved

Season word: *mukyūka* (Korean rose, rose of Sharon,

hibiscus syriacus; autumn)

The *mukyūka*, or *mugunghwa* in Korean, is the national

flower of Korea. This is based on the biographical novel

about the master of the tea ceremony, Sen no Rikyū (1522–

1591), *Rikyū ni tazune yo* (*lit.*, "Ask Rikyū", 2008) by

Yamamoto Ken'ichi (1956–2014).

白木槿

　　拉致者の生存

　　　　祈りたり

しろむくげ

　　らちしゃのせいぞん

　　　　いのりたり

季語　　白木槿（秋）

1970年代と1980年代に、北朝鮮は、486人の韓国人お
よび少なくとも17人の日本人を拉致し、スパイや通訳とし
て訓練した。2018年10月現在、ほとんどの拉致者の安否
は定かではない。

Shiro mukuge

    rachi sha no seizon

      inori tari

The white mukuge

    is praying

      that the abductees by North Korea are alive

Season word: *mukuge* (*hibiscus syriacus*; autumn)

The North Korean government abducted as many as 486

South Koreans, as well as at least 17 Japanese citizens in

the 1970s and 1980s. They were trained as spies and

language instructors. The whereabouts of most of them are

still unknown as of October 2018.

酔芙蓉

　　午前と午後の

　　　風誘ふ

すいふよう

　　ごぜんとごごの

　　　かぜさそう

季語　酔芙蓉（秋）

酔芙蓉の花は、午前中は白いが、午後になると、ピンク色
に変わるので、この名前がつけられた。

Sui fuyō

gozen to gogo no

kaze sasou

The drunken cotton rosemallow

is inviting the wind

in the morning and the afternoon

Season word: *sui fuyō* (*lit.*, "drunken cotton rosemallow,"

or *hibiscus mutabilis cv. versicolor*; autumn)

The flower of *sui fuyō* ("drunken cotton rosemallow") is

white in the morning but turns to pink in the afternoon;

hence the name.

朝露に

　　　露草の青

　　　　　溢れたり

あさつゆに

　　つゆくさのあお

　　こぼれたり

季語　露（秋）　露草（ツユクサ、秋）

別名は、青花（あおばな）、蛍草（ほたるぐさ）など。古名は、月草（つきくさ）。こぼれ種からよく繁殖するので、北米東部では厄介な雑草とみなされている。

Asa tsuyu ni

    tsuyu kusa no ao

        kobore tari

In the morning dew

    the dayflower is dropping

        its blue

Season words: *tsuyu* (dew; autumn) and *tsuyu kusa*
(Asiatic dayflower; autumn)
This tiny flower blooms only for one day. It is also called
ao bana (*lit.*, "blue flower") for its bright blue color and is
used for dyeing. The plant self-seeds and spreads rapidly
and is regarded as a weed in eastern North America.

鳳仙花

　　乙女心の

　　　色染めし

ほうせんか

　　おとめごころの

　　　いろそめし

季語　鳳仙花（秋）

鳳仙花は、染指草、爪紅（ツマベニ、ツマクレナイ）とも言われるように、昔は爪を染めるのに使われた。種は弾けて勢いよく飛び、こぼれ種でもよく生える。

Hōsenka

    otome gokoro no

        iro someshi

The touch-me-not

    paints the sensitive heart of

        the maiden

Season word: *hōsenka* (touch-me-not, rose balsam,

impatiens balsamina; autumn)

The red variety of this flower was used by girls to paint

their nails. The ripe seed capsules pop (which is called

'explosive dehiscence'); hence the name "touch-me-not."

秋桜

　　　花の数式

　　　　　究めたり

あきざくら

　　　はなのすうしき

　　　　　きわめたり

季語　　秋桜（アキザクラ、コスモス、秋）

花の数式とは、イタリアの数学者レオナルド・フィボナッチ（1175年頃–1250年頃）が、解明した数式、「フィボナッチ数」に基く花の数式のこと。

Aki zakura

hana no sūshiki

kiwame tari

The cosmos

is studying

the mathematical formula of flowers

Season word: *aki zakura* (cosmos; autumn)

The mathematical formula of flowers refers to an

application in nature of the Fibonacci sequence that was

discovered by the Italian mathematician, Leonardo de Pisa

or Fibonacci (c. 1175–c. 1250). The number of petals of

many flowers follows the Fibonacci sequence.

コスモスや

　　宇宙の果てを

　　　　垣間見る

コスモスや

　　うちゅうのはてを

　　　　かいまみる

季語　コスモス（秋）

Kosumosu ya

uchū no hate o

kaima miru

The cosmos

caught a glimpse

of the edge of the universe

Season word: *kosumosu* (cosmos; autumn)

秋海棠

　　思索に耽る

　　　　白き風

しゅうかいどう

　　しさくにふける

　　　　しろきかぜ

季語　秋海棠（秋）

Shūkaidō

shisaku ni fukeru

shiroki kaze

The hardy begonia

is absorbed in meditation

in the white wind

Season word: *shūkaidō* (hardy begonia; autumn)

萩の花

　　　平等院の

　　　　　女官なり

はぎのはな

　　　びょうどういんの

　　　　　にょかんなり

季語　萩の花（秋）

京都府宇治市にある平等院では、紫色の萩の花が慎まし

くも美しく咲く。

Hagi no hana

    Byōdō in no

        nyokan nari

The Japanese clover

    is the lady-in-waiting

        at the Byōdō-in

Season word: *hagi no hana* (Japanese clover, bush clover,

lespedeza; autumn)

The Byōdō-in in Uji, Kyoto prefecture, has beautiful

gardens with flowers in all seasons, including gentle and

graceful purple Japanese clover.

白桔梗

　　すれ違ふ想ひ

　　　白き露

しろききょう

　　すれちがうおもい

　　　しろきつゆ

季語　白桔梗（秋）　露（秋）

Shiro kikyō

sure chigau omoi

shiroki tsuyu

The white balloon flower

is thinking about the misunderstanding

and the white dew forms on it

Season words: *shiro kikyō* (white balloon flower; autumn)

and *tsuyu* (dew; autumn)

October

Photograph 10. Pink-edged white chrysanthemums, taken

by the author

異邦人

　　川和の菊の

　　　　迎へたり

いほうじん

　　かわわのきくの

　　　　むかえたり

季語　　菊（秋）

神奈川県横浜市都筑（つづき）区川和町（かわわちょう）は、

江戸時代、文政年間の頃から菊の栽培で知られ、現在も

「川和の菊」と呼ばれる豪商の旧家が残る。イライザ・シド

モア（1856年−1928年）は、『シドモア日本紀行　明治の

人力車ツアー』（原本、*Jinrikisha Days in Japan*、

1891年）で、「川和の菊」を紹介している。

Ihōjin

> Kawawa no kiku no
>
> mukae tari

The foreign visitor

> is welcomed
>
> > by the famed chrysanthemum in Kawawa

Season word: *kiku* (chrysanthemum; autumn)

In the mid-1880s, Eliza Ruhamah Scidmore (1856–1928)

visited Kawawa, in current Tuzuki ward, Yokohama,

Kanagawa prefecture, known for the horticulture of

chrysanthemum, and admired its beauty. She wrote about

it in *Jinrikisha Days in Japan* (1891).

シドモア女史

　　菊のサラダの

　　　　おもてなし

シドモアじょし

　　きくのサラダの

　　　　おもてなし

季語　菊(秋)

イライザ・シドモアは、神奈川県の川和で菊の花のサラダ
を初めて食し、その繊細な味を堪能した。

Shidomoa joshi

    kiku no sarada

        no omotenashi

Ms. Scidmore

    was treated to

        the chrysanthemum flower salad

Season word: *kiku* (chrysanthemum; autumn)

Eliza Ruhamah Scidmore tasted chrysanthemum flowers
for the first time in Kawawa, Kanagawa. She enjoyed both
the beauty and the subtle flavor of chrysanthemum salad.

曼珠沙華

　　刑場跡の

　　　　名残かな

まんじゅしゃげ

　　けいじょうあとの

　　　　なごりかな

季語　曼珠沙華（彼岸花、秋）

Manjushage

    keijō ato no

        nagori kana

The red spider lily

    is the reminder

        of the old execution grounds

Season word: *manjushage* (red spider lily; autumn)

The red spider lily blankets the old execution grounds of medieval times. This plant, with striking red flowers, is also known as an autumn equinox flower.

無縁墓

　　野菊の精の

　　　　宿りたり

むえんばか

　　のぎくのせいの

　　　　やどりたり

季語　野菊（秋）

Muen baka

   nogiku no sei no

      yadori tari

In the grave of the unknown persons

   dwell

      the souls of the wild chrysanthemums

Season word: *nogiku* (wild chrysanthemum; autumn)

講堂の蔦

　　聴講生に

　　　　なりすまし

こうどうのつた

　　ちょうこうせいに

　　　　なりすまし

　　　　　・

季語　蔦（秋）

Kōdō no tsuta

    chōkōsei ni

        nari sumashi

The ivy by the auditorium

    pretends to be

        an auditor of the class

Season word: *tsuta* (ivy; autumn)

蔦葛

　　鴎外門の

　　　　老門番

つたかずら

　　おうがいもんの

　　　　ろうもんばん

季語　蔦葛（秋）

作家の森鴎外（1862年－1922年）は、陸軍軍医総監でも

あり、晩年は、帝室博物館総長を務め、帝国奈良博物館

（現在の奈良国立博物館、正倉院宝物などの国宝を管理

する）を監督するため、奈良に転勤した。当時鴎外の住ん

だ官舎の門は「鴎外門」として保存されている。

Tsuta kazura

    Ōgai mon no

        rō monban

The ivy vine

    is the venerable guardian

        of the Ōgai Gate

Season word: *tsuta kazura* (ivy vine; autumn)

The surgeon-general and writer Mori Ōgai (1862–1922) in his

later years served as director-general of the Imperial Household

Museum and lived in Nara in order to oversee the Nara Imperial

Museum, which preserved the national treasures of Shōsō-in.

The wooden gate of his government residence still stands today,

which is referred to as the Ōgai Gate.

蔦葛

　　最期の一葉

　　　　風の止む

つたかずら

　　さいごのひとは

　　　　かぜのやむ

季語　蔦葛（秋）

米作家、オー・ヘンリー（1862年−1910年）の『最後の一葉』へのオマージュ。

Tsuta kazura

    saigo no hitoya

       kaze no yamu

The ivy vine

    has only its last leaf

       and the wind stops

Season word: *tsuta kazura* (ivy vine; winter)

This is a homage to *The Last Leaf* written by O. Henry
(1862–1910).

大楓

　　想ひ想ひに

　　　　装ひて

おおかえで

　　おもいおもいに

　　　　よそおいて

季語　　楓（秋）

大楓には、同じ枝に赤や黄色、オレンジ色に紅葉するもの
がある。緑の葉と混じって色のコントラストが美しい。

Ō kaede

omoi omoi ni

yoso oi te

The big maple

its leaves have put on colors

of its own liking for each

Season word: *kaede* (maple; autumn)

The leaves on a branch of a maple tree sometimes turn

different colors, such as orange, red, and yellow.

八幡宮

　　大銀杏のみ知る

　　　秋の風

はちまんぐう

　　おおいちょうのみしる

　　　あきのかぜ

季語　秋の風（秋）

神奈川県鎌倉市の八幡宮は、大銀杏の木で有名。銀杏（イチョウ）の木自体は、季語ではない。銀杏（ギンナン、イチョウの実）は秋の季語となる。

Hachiman gū

    ō ichō nomi shiru

       aki no kaze

At Hachiman Shrine

    only the grand ginko tree knows

       the autumn wind of long ago

Season word: *aki no kaze* (autumn wind; autumn)

A ginko (pronounced as "ichō") as a tree is not a season word,

whereas a gingo nut (the same characters as the ginko tree but

pronounced as "gin'nan") is a season word of autumn. Tsuruoka

Hachiman-gū is a famous shrine in Kamakura, Kanagawa

prefecture, patronized by Minamoto no Yoritomo (1147–1199)

and is known for its 1,000-year-old grand ginko tree.

篠懸の

　　　実のポンポン

　　　　　風踊る

すずかけの

　　　みのポンポン

　　　　　かぜおどる

季語　　篠懸の実（秋）

Suzukake no

    mi no pon pon

        kaze odoru

The plane tree nuts

    are like pom-poms

        and dance with the wind

Season word: *suzukake no mi* (berries of the plane tree,

platanus orientalis; autumn)

November

Photograph 11. Winter cherry blossoms with background

of fall foliage, taken by the author

姫胡桃

　　くるみ割り人形

　　　観劇す

ひめぐるみ

　　くるみわりにんぎょう

　　　かんげきす

季語　胡桃（秋）

冬の劇場の定番、チャイコフスキー（1840年−1893年）

作曲のバレエ音楽『くるみ割り人形』（作品71）によるバレ

エ作品に寄せて。

Hime gurumi

Kurumi wari ningyō

kangeki su

The little walnut

is watching

the Nutcracker

Season word: *hime gurumi* (a smaller species of Japanese

walnut; autumn)

The Nutcracker refers to the popular ballet to the music

composed by Peter Ilich Tchaikovsky (1840–1893).

石蕗の花

　　鴎外の森

　　　　想ひたり

つわぶきのはな

　　おうがいのもり

　　　　おもいたり

季語　　石蕗の花（冬）

森鷗外（1862年−1922年）は、石見国津和野（現在の島根県津和野町）で生まれた。津和野の語源は、「ツワブキの野」に由来する。石蕗は、冬に黄色の小花を咲かせる。

Tsuwabuki no hana

   Ōgai no mori

      omoi tari

The tsuwabuki flower

   is reminiscing about

      the wood of Ōgai

Season word: *tsuwabuki no hana* (flower of the leopard

plant, *farfugium japoicum*; winter)

Mori, surname of the surgeon-general and writer Mori Ōgai

(1862–1922), means wood. He was born in Tsuwano,

Shimane prefecture. Tsuwano means the field of *tsuwabuki*

that blooms with dainty yellow flowers in winter.

石蕗の花

　　『舞姫』の

　　　　涙見る

つわぶきのはな

　　まいひめの

　　　　なみだみる

季語　石蕗の花（冬）

森鴎外の代表作の一つ、『舞姫』（1890年）は、半自伝的

小説である。

Tsuwabuki no hana

   Mai hime no

      namida miru

The leopard plant flower

   saw

      the tears of the Dancing Girl

Season word: *tsuwabuki no hana* (flower of the leopard plant; winter)

Mori Ōgai wrote the semi-autobiographical novel, *Mai hime* (The Dancing Girl, 1890), the tragic love story of a young Japanese man who studied medicine in Germany in the mid-1880s and a German girl.

忘れ花

　　懐紙にそっと

　　　　忍ばせて

わすればな

　　かいしにそっと

　　　　しのばせて

季語　忘れ花（冬）

忘れ花は、季節外れの冬に咲く花のこと。

Wasure bana

kaishi ni sotto

shinobase te

The forgotten flower

is being tucked gently

in Japanese tissue paper

Season word: *wasure bana* (*lit.*, "forgotten flower," the

flower with unseasonable blooming in winter; winter)

Kaishi is traditional Japanese tissue paper, tucked inside the

upper part of a kimono.

忘れ花

　　齢重ねて

　　　　齢忘る

わすればな

　　よわいかさねて

　　　　としわする

季語　忘れ花（冬）

忘れ花は、季節外れの冬に咲く花。

Wasure bana

yowai kasane te

toshi wasuru

The forgotten flower

the woman had aged

and she has forgotten her age

Season word: *wasure bana* (*lit.*, "forgotten flower," the
flower with unseasonable blooming in winter; winter)

冬薔薇

　　凛と一輪

　　　　冬の空

ふゆそうび

　　りんといちりん

　　　　ふゆのそら

季語　冬薔薇（ふゆそうび、冬）　冬（冬）

Fuyu sōbi

   rin to ichirin

      fuyu no sora

The winter rose

   blooms alone gracefully and nobly

      in the winter sky

Season words: *fuyu sōbi* (winter rose; winter) and *fuyu*

(winter; winter)

冬の薔薇

　　女王の心

　　　　溶かしたり

ふゆのばら

　　じょおうのこころ

　　　　とかしたり

季語　　冬の薔薇（冬）

ハンス・クリスチャン・アンデルセン（1805年−1875年）の
童話、『雪の女王』からの連想。

Fuyu no bara

    joō no kokoro

        tokashi tari

The winter rose

    has melted the heart

        of the Snow Queen (and broke the spell)

Season word: *fuyu no bara* (winter rose; winter)

This loosely alludes to the fairy tale, *The Snow Queen*, by
Hans Christian Andersen (1805–1875).

お百度を

　　踏む足を看る

　　　　お茶の花

おひゃくどを

　　ふむあしをみる

　　　　おちゃのはな

季語　茶の花(冬)

O hyakudo o

    fumu ashi o miru

        o cha no hana

The tea blossom

    is watching over the feet of the woman

        offering the 100-prayer at the shrine

Season word: *cha no hana* (tea blossom; winter)

The tea bush blooms with white camellia-like flowers in winter. O-hyakudo (*lit.*, "one hundred times") refers to a form of prayer going back and forth in the approach to the shrine a hundred times and offering a prayer at the shrine a hundred times so that one's wish will come true.

寒桜

　　乳母車押す

　　　　手の寒し

かんざくら

　　うばぐるまおす

　　　　てのさむし

季語　寒桜(冬)　寒い(冬)

Kan zakura

uba guruma osu

te no samushi

The winter cherry blossom

feels the cold of the hands

that push the baby stroller

Season words: *kan zakura* (winter-blooming cherry;

winter) and *samui* (cold, winter)

柊の

　　　小花薫りて

　　　　　刺見張る

ひいらぎの

　　　こばなかおりて

　　　　　とげみはる

季語　　柊の花（冬）

柊（ひいらぎ）は、冬に白い芳香のある小花が咲き、春に
実がなる。それに対し、西洋ヒイラギは春に白い小花が咲
き、冬に実がなる。

Hiiragi no

kobana kaori te

toge miharu

The fragrant holly osmanthus

has bloomed

and its thorn is on guard

Season word: *hiiragi* (holly osmanthus, Chinese holly,

holly olive; winter)

The holly osmanthu blooms with fragrant, dainty white

flowers in winter and bear fruits in summer. By contrast,

common holly (English holly) blooms in spring and bears

fruits in winter.

December

Photograph 12. Sazanka (sasanqua), "Sazanka," January

21, 2006, under Creative Commons license,

https://commons.wikimedia.org/wiki/File:Sazanka_06a057

3s.jpg

実南天

　　　クリスマス・リースに

　　　　早変はり

みなんてん

　　　クリスマス・リースに

　　　　はやがわり

季語　　実南天（冬）

実南天で自家製のクリスマス・リースを作り、玄関のドアに
飾る。

Mi nanten

    Kurisumasu tsurii ni

        haya gawari

The heavenly bamboo with red berries

    has quickly turned

        into a Christmas wreath

Season word: *mi nanten* (heavenly bamboo with red berries; winter)

The evergreen shrub *nanten* (*lit.*, "southern heaven," heavenly bamboo, *nandina domestica*) is not a bamboo despite its English name.

寒椿

　　また山茶花と

　　　　間違へられる

かんつばき

　　またさざんかと

　　　　まちがえられる

季語　寒椿（冬）　山茶花（冬）

椿は、開花しても花は完全には開ききらず、花が散る時は、
花ごとポトリと落ちる。一方、山茶花は、花は完全に開き、
散る時は、花びらが一枚ずつ落ちる。

Kan tsubaki

mata sazanka to

machigae rareru

The winter camellia

is mistaken for sasanqua

again

Season words: *kan tsubaki* (winter camellia; winter) and

sazanka (sasanqua; winter)

The Japanese camellia in general does not open its flower

completely when it blooms, and falls as a whole, not petal

by petal. By contrast, sasanqua, a species of the Japanese

camellia, opens its flower wide and falls petal by petal.

冬椿

　　花神とともに

　　　　落ちにけり

ふゆつばき

　　かしんとともに

　　　　おちにけり

季語　冬椿（冬）

Fuyu tsubaki

kashin to tomoni

ochini keri

The winter camellia

has fallen

along with the spirit of the flower

Season word: *fuyu tsubaki* (winter camellia; winter)

山茶花や

　　姿勢正して

　　　　茶筅視る

さざんかや

　　しせいただして

　　　　ちゃせんみる

季語　山茶花(冬)

Sazanka ya

    shisei tadashite

        chasen miru

The sasanqua

    sits straight

        and observes the tea whisk intently

Season word: *sazanka* (sasanqua; winter)

This describes a scene of the traditional tea ceremony in winter, with a sasanqua flower arrangement in the tea ceremony room.

寒椿

　　独りで愛でる

　　　　寒の月

かんつばき

　　ひとりでめでる

　　　　かんのつき

季語　寒椿（冬）寒の月（冬）

Kan tsubaki

hitori de mederu

kan no tsuki

The winter camellia

is admiring the winter moon

alone

Season words: *kan tsubaki* (winter camellia; winter) and

kan no tsuki (winter moon; winter)

雪吊や

　　番を待つ

　　松の静けさ

ゆきつりや

　　ばんをまつ

　　まつのしづけさ

季語　雪吊（冬）

石川県金沢市にある兼六園の松の雪吊は冬の風物詩。

Yuki tsuri ya

    ban o matsu

        matsu no shizukesa

The snow rope hanging

    the pine trees are waiting

        their turns quietly

Season word: *yuki tsuri* (*lit.*, "snow rope hanging"; winter)

Yuki tsuri refers to the practice of hanging ropes from a bamboo

pole in a cone-shape, like an umbrella frame, in order to protect

pine trees from the weight of snow. The Kenroku Garden in

Kanazawa, Ishikawa prefecture, one of the three greatest gardens

in Japan, is famous for the *yuki tsuri*, which adds a distinctive

serenity to the winter landscape.

松と雪

　　下弦の月と

　　　　話したり

まつとゆき

　　かげんのつきと

　　　　はなしたり

季語　雪(冬)

Matsu to yuki

    kagen no tsuki to

        hanashi tari

The pine tree and snow

    are talking

        to the waning moon

Season word: *yuki* (snow; winter)

冬牡丹

　　藁のぼつちと

　　　　冬籠り

ふゆぼたん

　　わらのぼっちと

　　　　ふゆごもり

季語　冬牡丹（冬）　冬籠り（冬）

藁のぼつち（藁ぼっち）は、冬に植物などを寒さや雪から保護する藁の囲い。

Fuyu botan

    wara no bocchi to

      fuyu gomori

The winter peony

    is wrapped in the straw cape

      and is wintering

Season words: *fuyu botan* (winter tree peony; winter) and *fuyu gomoi* (wintering; winter)

Tokugawa Garden in Nagoya, Aichi prefecture, tends its prized tree peonies during the winter by wrapping each of them with a straw enclosure that looks like a large cape. The peony blossoms in winter please the visitors' eyes and hearts.

葉牡丹の

　　真白き寝間着

　　　　月の笑む

はぼたんの

　　ましろきねまき

　　　　つきのえむ

季語　葉牡丹(冬)

庭の葉牡丹が、雪にすっぽり覆われている様子。

Ha botan no

    mashiroki nemaki

        tsuki no emu

The ornamental kale

    has put on pure white pajamas

        and the moon smiles

Season word: *ha-botan* (*lit.*, "leaf peony," ornamental kale; winter)

This describes a scene in which ornamental kale in a garden is totally covered with snow.

湖の風

　　枯葉の

　　　　スケーターズ・ワルツ

うみのかぜ

　　かれはの

　　　　スケーターズ・ワルツ

季語　　枯葉（冬）

フランスの作曲家、エミール・ワルトトイフェル（1837年−
1915年）の『スケーターズ・ワルツ』（作品183）に寄せて。

Umi no kaze

kareha no

Sukētāzu warutsu

With the wind on the frozen lake

the dead leaves are dancing

the Skaters' Waltz

Season word: *kareha* (dead leaves; winter)

The Skaters' Waltz, Op. 183, was composed by French composer Émile Waldteufel (1837–1915).

About the author

Mayumi Itoh is a former Professor of Political Science at the University of Nevada, Las Vegas (UNLV). She has also taught at Princeton University and Queens College, City University of New York (CUNY), and has written more than 15 single-authored books, as well as more than 15 articles in professional journals. Her book titles include:

–*Globalization of Japan: Japanese Sakoku Mentality and U.S. Efforts to Open Japan* (1998)

–*The Hatoyama Dynasty: Japanese Political Leadership Through the Generations* (2003)

–*Japanese War Orphans in Manchuria: Forgotten Victims of World War II* (2010)

–*Japanese Wartime Zoo Policy: The Silent Victims of World War II* (2010)

–*The Origin of Ping-Pong Diplomacy: The Forgotten Architect of Sino-U.S. Rapprochement* (2011)

–Pioneers of Sino-Japanese Relations: Liao and Takasaki (2012)

–Hachi: The Truth of the Life and Legend of the Most Famous Dog in Japan (2013)

–The Origins of Contemporary Sino-Japanese Relations: Zhou Enlai and Japan (2016)

–The Making of China's War with Japan: Zhou Enlai and Zhang Xueliang (2016)

–The Making of China's Peace with Japan: What Xi Jinping Should Learn from Zhou Enlai (2017)

–"Hachi-ko" in Siberia: The True Story of Japanese Prisoners of War and a Dog (2017)

–Hachiko: Solving Twenty Mysteries about the Most Famous Dog in Japan (2017)

–Eliza Ruhamah Scidmore and Japan: The Life and Journeys to the Far East of the American Woman Who Brought "Sakura" to Washington, D.C. (2017)

–Kaneko Misuzu: Life and Poems of A Lonely Princes (2018)

–The Japanese Culture of Mourning Whales: Whale Graves and Memorial Monuments in Japan (2018)

–Haikus of All Seasons I: The Heavens and the Earth (2018)

–Animals and the Fukushima Nuclear Disaster (2018)

–Haikus of All Seasons II: Humanity (2018)

–Haikus of All Seasons III: Fauna (2018)

www.ingramcontent.com/pod-product-compliance
Lightning Source LLC
Chambersburg PA
CBHW051248250726
48656CB00004B/1183